GAMES FOR ALL YEAR

100 Games for SUMMER

BARRON'S

All inquiries should be addressed to:
Barron's Educational Series, Inc.
250 Wireless Boulevard
Hauppauge, New York 11788
http://www.barronseduc.com

International Standard Book No.: 0-7641-1754-8
Library of Congress Catalog Card No.: 00-064157

Library of Congress Cataloging-in-Publication Data
Allué, J. M. (Josep Maria)
   [Juegos para todo el año. English]
   Games for all year / J. M. Allué.
     p. cm.
   Includes bibliographical references and index.
   Contents: [v. 1] Games for summer
   ISBN 0-7641-1754-8 (v. 1)
     1. Games.   I. Title.
  GV1201 .A54 2001
  790.1—dc21

                                            00-064157

Printed in Spain
987654321

Contents

To Parents and Educators

Game playing is an innate activity and part of human nature. Its importance in our physical and intellectual development contributes to making game playing an essential part of childhood and in sustaining our interest in games throughout our lives. The spontaneity, pleasure, and joy involved in playing games helps children establish interpersonal relationships and have fun with family, friends, and classmates, regardless of the age or gender of the players.

When we talk about games, we usually refer to a series of activities that are carried out freely for the sole purpose of having fun. While it is true that our desire to play is inborn, what we play depends on the resources available at the moment, such as space, number of players, materials, and familiarity with specific games.

In this respect, games can be orchestrated and, knowing their importance in the physical and intellectual development of young children, resources must be made available for offering children a variety of new and appealing games that encourage them to explore, have fun, and interact with others and their surroundings.

Playing means fun and entertainment. In *Games for Summer* we offer **100** different games whose only requirement from you is a desire to play them!

Games for Summer

The arrival of summer, with school out and summer vacation underway, means lots of free time for children. So much leisure time makes games all the more important for keeping children occupied during the day.

In summer, children spend a lot of time at day camps and sleep-away camps, thus making outdoor games more common during this season than during any other. The summer heat also encourages visits to the beach and pool, places that offer special environments for playing and having fun.

Although summer is the perfect time for playing outdoor games, other less active games are needed for those times when we take car or train trips, or when we want to spend relaxing moments after dinner.

The games in this book are divided into five sections. Each game begins with information about the target age range, the recommended time it takes to play the game, the approximate number of players, the materials needed, and the level of activity involved in each game. Following are the sections included in *Games for Summer*:

- **Games for the Park:** People play in the park more in summer than in any other season. This section presents a series of outdoor games designed to provide a fun-filled afternoon without ever having to leave the city.

- **Travel Games:** To avoid boredom on long summer trips when we are confined to a closed space, this section offers a series of entertaining games that can be played without having to move around much. All that is needed to play these games are our minds and powers of observation. The games can also be used for other times of leisure.

- **Beach Games:** Trips to the beach are among children's favorite activities. This section describes a variety of games that are played both in and out of the water. It includes high- and low-activity games and those played in teams and pairs. All of the games entail a lot of fun.

- **Pool Games:** The hot temperatures in summer encourage frequent trips to the pool with family and friends. There the main activity of both children and adults is playing in the water. The games in this section will appeal to people of all ages.

- **Team Games:** Summer camps make it easy to find friends eager for an afternoon of fun and entertainment. The team games provided in this section offer exciting ways to make the most of this situation.

Games for All Year

The collection *Games for All Year* compiles **400** games divided into four volumes, one for each season of the year: *Spring*, *Summer*, *Fall*, and *Winter*. Each volume presents **100** games selected on the basis of the play area appropriate for individual seasons. The games have been classified this way to make it easier to select a particular game and to get it started quickly. However, all of the games can be played at any time of the year as long as you have the desire to play them and the time to do so.

J. M. Allué

Games

1

for the park

The park is a place that offers everything one needs to spend an entire afternoon having fun. Open spaces, friends, and time off from school all contribute to making it possible to enjoy oneself close to home.

25 outdoor games using slides, benches, and open spaces for playing various games of tag, hide-and-seek, and water games when temperatures soar. Mothers, fathers, baby-sitters, and others will find in this section games that make going to the park a favorite pastime for children.

1 Water Carrier

In this game, players have to finish a race with a cup of water on their head. A game leader indicates the course.

- **Age:** 4 years and up
- **Approximate Time:** 10 minutes
- **Players:** 2 or more
- **Materials:** 1 plastic cup per player, water
- **Activity Level:** average

1. Players stand at a designated line and use one hand to hold a cup of water on their head. An adult will serve as game leader.

2. The game begins with the leader shouting "Go!" At the signal, players start to walk, holding the cup on their head and trying to keep the water from spilling.

3. As players advance, the game leader indicates the course with phrases such as "to the tree!," "hop three times on one foot," or "under the bench!"

4. The player who has spilled the least amount of water at the end of the game will give the orders for the next game's race.

2 The Water Slide

In this refreshing game, players need a lot of balance to come down the slide.

- **Age:** 5 years and up
- **Approximate Time:** 5 minutes
- **Players:** 2 or more
- **Materials:** 1 plastic plate per player, water, a slide
- **Activity Level:** average

1. An adult will serve as game leader. Each player receives a plastic plate and fills it with water. Players then line up behind the slide.

2. The leader holds the first player's plate while she climbs the steps. When the player gets to the top of the slide, the leader returns her plate.

3. The child has to come down the slide holding the plate out in front of her with both hands, trying not to spill the water.

4. If there is any water left on her plate when she gets to the bottom of the slide, the player gets back in line. The game continues until there is only one player left with water on her plate.

③ Balloon Fight

The object of this water balloon fight is not to tag players but to squirt them.

- **Age:** 5 years and up
- **Approximate Time:** 10 minutes
- **Players:** 4 or more
- **Materials:** 1 balloon per player, a whistle, a fountain
- **Activity Level:** high

1. Before starting the game, each player gets a balloon and fills it with water at a fountain or tap where an adult leader is standing.

2. After they fill their balloons, players go off to hide in the park. After five minutes, the leader blows a whistle to signal the beginning of the game.

3. Players can come out from their hiding places, or they can stay where they are and wait to surprise one of their companions. The object of the game is to squirt each other with the balloon.

4. When a player is squirted, she can turn around and wet her attacker. They continue in the "fight" until one of them retreats or runs out of water.

5. A player cannot be squirted when her balloon is empty or when she is in view of the game leader. The game ends when the leader blows the whistle again.

The Bench

Players try to get and keep a seat on the bench by pushing others off.

- **Age:** 5 years and up
- **Approximate Time:** 5 minutes
- **Players:** 7 or more
- **Materials:** a bench
- **Activity Level:** high

1. Players choose a bench to use for the game and stand a certain distance away from it. When one of the players gives the starting signal, everyone runs to the bench.

2. The players who get to the bench first sit down and the other players try to push them off.

3. When a player gets knocked off the bench, she goes to the other side and tries to push her way on again.

4. The game continues in this way with players pushing and sitting until they get tired, at which point the game ends.

Pass the Water

A fair amount of energy and speed are needed for this game in which children try to fill a bottle with water without getting wet in the process.

- **Age:** 6 years and up
- **Approximate Time:** 10 minutes
- **Players:** 5 or more
- **Materials:** 1 plastic cup per player, 2 plastic bottles per team, water
- **Activity Level:** low

1. Players divide into teams and sit in a single line on the floor, one behind the other. Each player holds a plastic cup in his or her hand.

2. The first player on each team has a full bottle of water. The last player has an empty bottle. At the signal, the first player fills her cup with water and, without turning around, empties it into the cup of the player behind her.

3. Players continue passing the water from cup to cup without turning around, until it reaches the last player, who then pours the water into the bottle. The game continues until the bottles of the two first players are empty.

4. The team that ends up with the most water in its bottle at the end of the game wins.

6 Bocce

This is a simplified version of a game commonly played in Italy and France. Other versions of this game are played throughout the world.

- **Age:** 6 years and up
- **Approximate Time:** 10 minutes
- **Players:** 2 or more
- **Materials:** 1 small ball (about $1\frac{1}{2}$ in. in diameter), 2 balls (about 3 in. in diameter) per player
- **Activity Level:** low

1. Players form two teams and draw straws to see which team will toss the small target ball. Then players designate a rectangular playing area and a toss line.

2. To begin, the first team tosses a small ball, which will be used as a target, into the rectangular area. Then they toss one of their other balls, trying to get one as close as possible to the target. Then play passes to the other team.

3. The second team tosses its balls, one at a time, aiming either at an opponent's ball or at the target. The object is to get one's own ball closer to the target than the opponent. Play then passes to the other team.

4. Teams continue taking turns until all of the balls have been tossed. The team that gets a ball closest to the target wins the game. The game is played for the number of rounds decided beforehand.

7 Elastic Ropes

This game using elastic ropes originated in China and is known by different names in other parts of the world.

- **Age:** 6 years and up
- **Approximate Time:** 10 minutes
- **Players:** 3 or more
- **Materials:** several elastic ropes
- **Activity Level:** average

1. Straws are drawn to see which two players will hold the ropes. The rest of the players line up in single file in front of them at the center.

2. When the game begins, players hold the elastic rope at ankle level. The other players take turns stepping on them so that the ropes lie on the ground.

3. After everyone has stepped on the ropes, players raise them to knee level. Again, players take turns stepping on them and bring them to the ground. If a player fails to do so, she is eliminated from the game.

4. Players continue to raise the ropes after each round until no one is able to step on them so that they touch the ground. The first two players eliminated from the game hold the ropes in the next one.

8 Limping Roosters

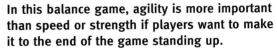

- **Age:** 6 years and up
- **Approximate Time:** 5 minutes
- **Players:** 2 or more
- **Materials:** none
- **Activity Level:** average

1. A flat, circular playing area is designated and players have to remain inside it as long as they are in the game. Players stand at the outside boundary of the playing area.

2. At the signal, players hop on one foot holding their arms crossed in front of them and move toward the center of the circle.

In this balance game, agility is more important than speed or strength if players want to make it to the end of the game standing up.

3. Players use their bodies to bump and knock others off balance, forcing them to touch the ground with their raised foot. Or they try to knock others out of the circle.

4. When a player puts her foot down or steps out of the circle, she is eliminated. The last player who survives on one foot in the circle wins the game.

9 Fill the Bucket

- **Age:** 6 years and up
- **Approximate Time:** 10 minutes
- **Players:** 10 or more
- **Materials:** 1 large bucket and 1 small bucket per team, 1 glass of water per team, a small stick, water
- **Activity Level:** average

1. Players divide into teams and fill a large bucket with water. Players on each team line up one behind the other around the bucket like spokes on a wheel.

2. The last player on each team gets a plastic cup and a small bucket. She places the empty bucket behind her on the ground

This game, which involves lots of splashing, refreshes and amuses all participants.

and, when the game begins, she passes the cup to the player in front of her.

3. Players continue passing the cup until it reaches the first player. That player fills the cup with water and bends down to pass it through his legs to the player behind him, who does the same.

4. When the cup reaches the last player, she empties it into her small bucket and returns the cup, repeating the process. The game ends when there is no more water left in the big bucket. The team that ends up with the most water in their small bucket wins.

10 Balloon Toss

In this exciting game, players pass a water balloon to each other from an increasingly wider distance.

- **Age:** 7 years and up
- **Approximate Time:** 5 minutes
- **Players:** 2 or more
- **Materials:** a balloon, water
- **Activity Level:** low

1. Players fill a balloon with water and tie it at the neck. Then they begin the game standing 3 feet apart.

2. The player with the balloon tosses it up to her companion, who tries to catch it without it breaking.

3. With each successful pass, players take a step backward so that they are standing farther away from each other, making the passes more difficult.

4. Players continue tossing the balloon until it breaks and wets one of them. The last player to toss the balloon will put a new balloon in play.

11 Pull the Stick

"Pull the Stick" is a game of strength that was first played by shepherds. The object is to pull the other player off the ground.

- **Age:** 7 years and up
- **Approximate Time:** 5 minutes
- **Players:** 2
- **Materials:** a strong stick about 20 inches long
- **Activity Level:** average

1. Two players sit facing each other with their legs extended in front of them and the soles of their feet against each other.

2. After they sit down, players grab the stick, closely alternating their hands.

3. At the signal, each player pulls the stick toward her with all her might, trying to lift her companion off the ground.

4. The first player to succeed in getting the other player to bend her knees or lift her bottom off the ground is the winner.

12 Speeding Hoop

In this amusing game, players practice their aim using a hoop and several empty cans.

Age: 7 years and up

Approximate Time: 10 minutes

Players: 2 or more

Materials: a hoop about 20 inches in diameter, as many empty soda cans as there are players less one

Activity Level: average

1. One player is chosen to toss the hoop. Each of the other players gets an empty can and stands in a line.

2. The player tossing the hoop stands about 9 feet from the line of players and rolls the hoop parallel to it.

3. As the hoop passes by, each player tries to toss his or her can through it and score a point.

4. Players continue tossing their cans until a score decided beforehand has been reached. If a player knocks the hoop over, he or she replaces the player rolling it.

13 Hide-and-Seek

"Hide-and-Seek" is one of the most widely known and popular games played by children, and the park is one of the best places to play it.

Age: 7 years and up

Approximate Time: 10 minutes

Players: 5 or more

Materials: none

Activity Level: average

1. Players draw straws to choose "It." They then designate a home base. "It" stays at home base, closes her eyes, and counts to a number players have decided on beforehand.

2. As "It" counts, the other players run off to hide. When "It" finishes counting, she yells "Ready or not, here I come!" and starts searching for the hiding players.

3. When "It" spots a player, she runs home to call out the player's name, for example, "One, two, three, Joshua!" The player "It" spots tries to reach home before "It" does.

4. To be safe, a player must reach home and shout "One, two, three, safe" before "It" calls out her name.

5. The game ends when all of the players have either been caught or are safe. The first one tagged is the new "It."

Barabú

Age: 7 years and up

Approximate Time: 10 minutes

Players: 5 or more

Materials: none

Activity Level: average

A game of hide-and-seek in which the players "It" tags have to help her find the others.

1. Players draw straws to choose "It." Then they establish the boundaries for the hiding area and decide how high "It" has to count.

2. "It" closes her eyes and counts to herself until she gets to the last five numbers, which she counts out loud. In the meantime, the other players run off to hide.

3. When "It" finishes counting, she starts to search for the other players. When she spots one, she tags and captures him. Players can't move until they are tagged.

4. Tagged players then join up with and help "It" find the others. However, only "It" can tag them.

5. When "It" and her helpers can't find anyone else, they shout "Barabú!" The hiding players shout back "Here!" to give the searchers a clue as to their whereabouts. The game ends when everyone has been caught.

15 Ball Catch

Age: 8 years and up

Approximate Time: 10 minutes

Players: 2 or more

Materials: a beach pail, a small rubber ball

Activity Level: average

In this game, which requires good coordination and reflexes, players have to catch a ball they have bounced themselves while it is still in the air.

1. Players designate an order of play and a bounce line. Then they line up in single file.

2. The first player puts the pail on the ground beside her and holds the ball in her hand. Then she bounces the ball out in front of her and tries to catch it with the pail.

3. If she succeeds, she marks the spot where she catches the ball and then passes the ball and the pail to the next player, who repeats the process. The second player tries to catch the ball a little farther out.

4. Each player marks the spot where she catches the ball, the object being to catch it as far out as possible.

16 Wounded, Grave, and Dead

The object of this fun, fast-paced game is to catch a pass without letting the ball drop.

Age: 8 years and up

Approximate Time: 10 minutes

Players: 4 or more

Materials: a ball

Activity Level: average

1. Players stand in a circle about 5 feet from each other. One player holds the ball in her hands.

2. The player who has the ball quickly passes it to one of the other players, who has to catch it without moving out of place. If the second player catches the ball, he passes it to someone else.

3. The first time a player drops the ball he is "wounded"; the second time, he is "grave"; and the third time, he is "dead." Dead players are out of the game.

4. The game continues until there are only two players left passing the ball.

17 Hoop Roll

This is an interesting game that our grandparents enjoyed as children.

- **Age:** 8 years and up
- **Approximate Time:** 10 minutes
- **Players:** 1 or more
- **Materials:** a hoop about 25 inches in diameter, a stick about 20 inches long and 1/2 inch thick per player
- **Activity Level:** average

1. A bicycle tire can be used for the hoop, or a hoop can be made by connecting the ends of a thin plastic tube about 6 feet long and 1 inch in diameter.

2. The player stands the hoop next to her and tries to make it roll using the stick.

3. The stick will help keep the hoop balanced by controlling its speed. This will take a lot of practice because at first the hoop will keep falling over.

4. When players are finally able to control the movement of the hoop, they can compete in races and relays on courses designated beforehand.

18 Bouncy Bounce

This is a game of coordination in which players have to keep the ball bouncing on the bottom of a bucket.

- **Age:** 8 years and up
- **Approximate Time:** 5 minutes
- **Players:** 1 or more
- **Materials:** a beach pail and a small rubber ball per player
- **Activity Level:** average

1. Each player receives a beach pail and a ball. Then they designate a course to follow during the game.

2. All of the players stand at the starting line holding the pail upside down and keeping the ball on its base.

3. At the sound of "Go!," players start to race, bouncing the ball on the bottom of the pail. If a player drops the ball, she has to stop and pick it up.

4. The first player to finish the course wins the game. Another way to determine the winner is to see who can achieve the most consecutive bounces, or who can bounce the ball the highest.

On to Rome

- **Age:** 9 years and up
- **Approximate Time:** 30 minutes
- **Players:** 8 or more
- **Materials:** a ball
- **Activity Level:** high

This team game, played in several parts of Spain, is a great way to burn energy while having fun at the same time.

1. Players form two teams. Two circles 6 feet in diameter are drawn on the ground 120 feet apart. One team stands inside one of the circles. The other team scatters between the two circles. One of the players passes the ball to a player inside the circle. This player then uses her hand to slap the ball as far as possible.

2. When the ball is hit, the first team runs to the other circle. Players on the second team try to catch the ball and tag their opponents with it.

3. If the second team tags a player outside of the circle, the teams switch roles. Otherwise, the first team scores a point. The game ends when one team reaches ten points.

A-E-I-O-U

- **Age:** 9 years and up
- **Approximate Time:** 5 minutes
- **Players:** 4 or more
- **Materials:** a ball
- **Activity Level:** average

In this game, players not only have to keep the ball in the air, but they also have to try to dodge it after they hear the last vowel in a series.

1. Players spread out but not too far from each other. One of the players throws the ball in the air and calls out "A!"

2. A player close to the ball smacks it up again and shouts "E!" Players are not allowed to grab the ball in any way, but must hit it with a flat hand.

3. The game continues in this way with players calling out vowels until they get to "U." The player who calls out "U!" tries to hit another player with the ball.

4. If she hits someone, that player is eliminated. If she fails to hit someone, she is eliminated. The player who stays in the game puts the ball back in play. The game ends when only one player is left.

21 Bottle Keeper

Good aim is required for this game, often played in the Spanish countryside. The object is to knock a bottle over and get away fast before the bottle keeper tags you.

- **Age:** 9 years and up
- **Approximate Time:** 30 minutes
- **Players:** 7 or more
- **Materials:** a ball, a plastic bottle, chalk
- **Activity Level:** average

1. Establish the playing area by drawing a boundary line with a circle 25 inches in diameter in the center. Place the bottle inside the circle and the bottle keeper next to it.

2. Draw a parallel line about 9 feet from the first one for players to stand on.

3. Players take turns tossing the ball and trying to knock the bottle down and out of the circle. If a player succeeds, she runs to get the ball and cross the boundary line with it.

4. When a player knocks the bottle down, the bottle keeper rushes to stand it up again in the circle and tag the player who knocked it over before that player crosses the boundary line with the ball.

5. If the player is tagged, she becomes the bottle keeper. If she gets across the boundary line, she scores a point. The game is played to 20 points.

22 Propeller

In this unusual game of tag, players try to tag each other from a push-up position and without moving their feet.

- **Age:** 9 years and up
- **Approximate Time:** 5 minutes
- **Players:** 2
- **Materials:** a hoop about 2 feet in diameter
- **Activity Level:** high

1. Players place the hoop on the ground and get in a push-up position, keeping their feet inside the hoop.

2. Players begin the game with the soles of their feet facing each other

and their bodies diametrically opposite.

3. At the signal, players try to tag the person to their right, making sure that their feet stay inside the circle.

4. The first player who succeeds in tagging the other is the winner.

23 Water Bowling

"Water Bowling" is a game in which players use a ball to knock their opponent's bottle of water over until it is empty.

- **Age:** 9 years and up
- **Approximate Time:** 10 minutes
- **Players:** 2 or more
- **Materials:** a ball, 2 plastic bottles, water
- **Activity Level:** high

1. Each player gets a bottle and fills it with water. Then players draw straws to see who will be the first to bowl. Players should stand about 15 feet apart.

2. Players place their bottles in front of them. Then they take turns rolling the ball, trying to knock over their opponent's bottle.

3. When a player's bottle is knocked over, she must hurry to retrieve the ball, and cannot stand her bottle up again until she has done so.

4. When no more water is left in a player's bottle, she is eliminated from the game. The game is played until only one bottle has water left.

24 Puzzle Hunt

- **Age:** 10 years and up
- **Approximate Time:** 30 minutes
- **Players:** 6 or more
- **Materials:** a piece of paper and pencil per team, scissors, a bucket
- **Activity Level:** average

1. Players divide into teams and draw a picture on a piece of paper. The game leader collects the drawings, cuts each into six pieces, and puts the pieces in the bucket.

2. Players stand 15 feet away from the bucket. At the signal, one member of each team runs to get a piece of paper. She then runs back to her group.

3. A player cannot take more than one piece of paper at a time, and she cannot look at

This is a fun game that combines speed, skill, and drawing. It is best for an adult to serve as game leader.

the paper until she gets back to her group. If the piece of paper does not belong to the other team's puzzle, the next player up returns it to the bucket. The object of the game is to be the first to complete the other team's puzzle.

25 Stealing Ground

- **Age:** 11 years and up
- **Approximate Time:** 10 minutes
- **Players:** 2 or more
- **Materials:** a spike about 8 inches long or an old screwdriver, chalk
- **Activity Level:** low

1. Mark a square on the ground and divide it into as many sections as there are players. Sections should be large enough for each player to stand in.

2. The first player stands in her own space and tries to fling the spike into the opponent's area. If she is successful, the dividing line is moved back to where the spike is, making her space larger.

3. The player continues flinging the spike and enlarging her territory as long as the spike sticks in the ground. When she misses, play passes to the other player, who then tries to regain his space.

This is an entertaining game, suitable for playing on soft ground. Caution should be used when flinging the spike.

4. Players who are not flinging the spike must stay outside of the square. A player is eliminated when her section becomes so small that it is impossible for her to stand in it even on tiptoes.

Travel

1oo

Games

Summer vacation can involve long trips by car or train and extended periods of time spent in confined spaces. This section includes a series of games that are designed to amuse and entertain while requiring little room to play.

15 travel games in which space is not an important consideration. Included here are observation games that require us to look out the window and notice our surroundings, word games that will stimulate our minds and enrich our vocabularies, and other games well-suited for trips and other relaxing moments.

Travel Magazine

This game is a wonderful way to pass the time while traveling in a car or train. It is played by looking out the window.

Age: 5 years and up

Approximate Time: 10 minutes

Players: 2 or more

Materials: a magazine and a pencil or marker for each player

Activity Level: low

1. Each player is given a magazine and a pencil or marker. An adult distributes the materials and leads the game.

2. Players look through their magazines for a specified amount of time, usually several minutes, noting the photos and other items in it.

3. When the time allotted for looking through the magazine is up, children look out the window trying to spot objects like those they saw in their magazines.

4. When a player spots an item she saw in her magazine, she says, for example, "I see a house like this one," and then shows everybody the corresponding picture.

5. Players make a pencil mark on all of the pictures of the items they spot. At the end of the game, the number of items each player checked off is added up to see how many items each player found.

Colors and Sizes

In this game of colors and sizes, players identify objects of the same color and name them in order.

- **Age:** 6 years and up
- **Approximate Time:** 5 minutes
- **Players:** 2 or more
- **Materials:** none
- **Activity Level:** low

1. Players establish an order of play so that when the last player has taken a turn, the first player begins again.

2. The first player picks a color, such as green. The second player sets a selection criterion for the objects: larger, smaller, or same size.

3. The third player starts the game by naming an object of the color mentioned. Then each player takes a turn to name a different object of that color.

4. If the size criterion chosen was "larger," each new object has to be larger than the previous one; if the size criterion was "smaller," then the object has to be smaller; if the criterion was "same size," then the object has to be the same size.

5. Players continue in this way with each series until they run out of objects or a player repeats an object.

28 Three Questions

This is a fun question-and-answer game that tests players' knowledge.

- **Age:** 6 years and up
- **Approximate Time:** 10 minutes
- **Players:** 2 or more
- **Materials:** none
- **Activity Level:** low

1. An order of play is established. Each player asks the player next to him questions. If that player cannot answer the question, or if she answers three questions correctly, play passes to the next player.

2. The first player asks the last player a question on a topic of common knowledge, such as animals, sports, or TV programs.

3. If that player answers correctly, the next player will ask her another question on the same topic. If she gets it right, the third player will ask her another question on the same topic. If she answers the third question correctly, she scores a point.

4. The first player to get five points wins the game. The difficulty of the questions will depend on the age of the players.

29 Alphabet Objects

Players look out the window to play this game, which will help pass the time on a car or train trip.

- **Age:** 6 years and up
- **Approximate Time:** 10 minutes
- **Players:** 2 or more
- **Materials:** none
- **Activity Level:** low

1. Players draw straws to see who will select a letter for the others. This player will say, for example, "What do you see that begins with 'A'?"

2. When the letter is given, all of the players look out the window to find objects that begin with that letter.

3. As soon as a player sees an object that begins with the letter, she calls it out and gets a point. The mentioned object cannot be repeated.

4. The player who names the most objects and has the most points when time is up wins the game and chooses the letter for the next game.

30 Palm Clap

- **Age:** 6 years and up
- **Approximate Time:** 5 minutes
- **Players:** 2
- **Materials:** none
- **Activity Level:** low

1. Two players face each other with open palms and bent arms. Palms should be at shoulder height.

2. One of the players will lead the game by saying "Right," "Left," or "Both," depending on the hands that have to be clapped.

3. When the leader says "Right," players clap their right hands together. If she says "Left," they clap their left hands; and

This is a game of coordination that is very appealing to children. It can also be played to the beat of a song.

when she says "Both," they clap both hands together.

4. The game leader speeds up the tempo as the game progresses.

31 Say It Again

- **Age:** 6 years and up
- **Approximate Time:** 10 minutes
- **Players:** 3 or more
- **Materials:** none
- **Activity Level:** low

This is a game of questions well-suited for long trips or situations where there is little room to move.

1. It is advisable for an adult to lead this game. Players will answer all together, or in pairs if there are a lot of players.

2. The leader will ask for information, for example, "Give me the names of fish, one, two, three, say it again."

3. Players take turns giving responses for a minute and a half, trying not to repeat any. If they make a mistake or repeat a response, they lose a turn.

4. One point is scored for each correct answer. Points are tallied at the end of the game.

32 Word Chain

A broad vocabulary and good memory are needed to keep the "Word Chain" going.

- **Age:** 6 years and up
- **Approximate Time:** 10 minutes
- **Players:** 2 or more
- **Materials:** none
- **Activity Level:** low

1. Players establish an order of play. After the last player has had a turn, the first player starts again.

2. The first player begins the game by saying the first word that comes to her mind, for example, "Dragon."

3. The next player has to say another word that begins with the last letter of the mentioned word, for example, "Nest." The next word has to begin with "T."

4. The game continues with players naming words until a player cannot continue or until a word is repeated.

33 Code

In this game, words are substituted for different sounds in a story developed by all players.

- **Age:** 7 years and up
- **Approximate Time:** 10 minutes
- **Players:** 2 or more
- **Materials:** none
- **Activity Level:** low

1. Players establish an order of play, and one of them begins to tell a story, for example, about friends who go on a trip.

2. Whenever she wishes, the first player can substitute one of the words with a sound, for example, "buzz" for "wheel." Then it is the next player's turn.

3. The next player adds to the story, but instead of saying "wheel" she uses the sound assigned to it by the first player.

4. Once a player has repeated all of the sounds, she can add another sound. Players continue repeating all the previous sounds, adding one of their own. The game ends when players cannot remember all of the sounds that have become part of the story.

What Should We Put in There?

In this rhyming game, players use their imaginations to place items into a container.

- **Age:** 7 years and up
- **Approximate Time:** 5 minutes
- **Players:** 2 or more
- **Materials:** none
- **Activity Level:** low

1. Players establish an order of play. The game begins with the first player asking the others a question: "What should we put in the refrigerator?"

2. The next player answers with a word that rhymes with "refrigerator"—"alligator," for example. Players should not worry if their answers don't make sense.

3. Players continue giving answers until they run out of rhyming words. The last person to give an answer makes up the next question.

4. With each question a new container or object that can hold things is named: a basket, a suitcase, a truck, a box, a house, and so on.

License Plates and Words

This is a good game to play on car trips. It uses the letters of car license plates.

- **Age:** 7 years and up
- **Approximate Time:** 10 minutes
- **Players:** 2 or more
- **Materials:** none
- **Activity Level:** low

1. Players draw straws to see who will go first. Then the first player looks for a license plate.

2. When she spots one, she spells out the letters aloud, for example, Y—A—P.

3. The other players try to make up a sentence using each letter as the first letter of each word in the sentence, for example, "You are puppies."

4. The first player able to come up with a sentence using the letters will look for the next license plate.

Words and Letters

In this easy game, players must make up words that begin with a particular letter.

- **Age:** 7 years and up
- **Approximate Time:** 5 minutes
- **Players:** 2 or more
- **Materials:** none
- **Activity Level:** low

1. Players determine an order of play. Then the first player chooses a letter and says aloud, for example, "Words that begin with . . . 'A'."

2. Each player takes a turn to say a word that begins with the letter chosen by the first player.

3. Players try to remember all of the words mentioned so they don't repeat any. A player who repeats a word is eliminated from the game.

4. The game ends when players cannot come up with any new words beginning with the chosen letter, or when all of the players have been eliminated.

Combined Letters

In this vocabulary game, players have fun while learning new words.

- **Age:** 8 years and up
- **Approximate Time:** 5 minutes
- **Players:** 2 or more
- **Materials:** none
- **Activity Level:** low

1. To begin, players take turns choosing at least four consonants, for example, S, P, L, C.

2. Then a time limit is established, usually 30 seconds, in which everyone has a chance to think about words that contain those consonants.

3. When time is up, each player calls out the words he came up with that contain all, or some, of the consonants. Examples of words for this case might be: "sock," "place," "special."

4. The player whose word has most of the consonants, in this case "special," scores a point. The game is played until at least five points are scored.

38 Dog, Cat, Mouse . . .

This game tests players' memory and knowledge. Besides coming up with their own answers, players have to remember all of the previous answers.

- **Age:** 8 years and up
- **Approximate Time:** 5 minutes
- **Players:** 2 or more
- **Materials:** none
- **Activity Level:** low

1. Players establish an order of play. When the last player has taken her turn, the first player starts again. The first player starts the game by naming a category, for example, names of animals.

2. In turn, each player calls out the name of an animal, but before doing so, she must repeat, in order, the names of all of the animals that were mentioned before.

3. Therefore, if "goat," "dog," "deer," and "mouse" have been named, the player whose turn it is has to mention all of them before adding a new one, for example, "cat."

4. When a player makes a mistake in the order of the words, or cannot add a new word to the list, she is eliminated from the game.

39 Line of Letters

In "Line of Letters," the challenge consists of forming the longest sequence of words. The game proceeds continuously from one word to the other.

- **Age:** 9 years and up
- **Approximate Time:** 10 minutes
- **Players:** 2 or more
- **Materials:** none
- **Activity Level:** low

1. Players decide on an order of play. The first player will start again after the last one has played. The first player begins by calling out any word, for example, "sun."

2. The next player has to call out another word that begins with the first letter of this word, such as "star."

3. The third player must call out a word that begins with the first two letters of the previous word, such as "stick."

4. The next player has to say a word that begins with the first three letters of the previous word and add one more, for example, "stir." The process continues with the next player who might say "stirrup," and so on.

5. When a round ends, the player who gave the last word starts a new game by choosing another word. Players note how many words they can build in each round.

License Plate Contest

This is a very relaxing game that can last for several days and span over different trips.

- **Age:** 9 years and up
- **Approximate Time:** 30 minutes
- **Players:** 2 or more
- **Materials:** none
- **Activity Level:** low

1. At the beginning of the road trip, the game rules and the kinds of license plates that will be looked for are established. During the trip, other games can be played at the same time this game is played.

2. The types of plates that are usually looked for are the plates with the "highest number," "smallest number," "most repeated numbers," "most numbers in a row," and so on.

3. When a player spots a license plate that beats the ones already called out, she points it out and scores a point. If another player spots a plate that beats the last one at a later time during the trip, the point of the previous player is nullified.

4. At the end of the trip, each player announces the categories in which she has earned a point; even though the trip has ended, the game can continue to be played on the next road trip.

Games

Trips to the beach offer a special opportunity for playing a variety of games. The games in this section make time spent at the beach more enjoyable by presenting games to be played in the water, on the beach, and with sand. Some of the games involve a lot of action; others do not.

26 games for playing at the beach and making the most of what the beach has to offer. Games are played in the water and on sand, where one can have fun digging, building, and tracing. All of the games played in the water should be supervised by an adult.

Penguin Race

This is a simple and amusing game children can play on the beach or before they undress to go into the water.

- **Age:** 4 years and up
- **Approximate Time:** 5 minutes
- **Players:** 2 or more
- **Materials:** none
- **Activity Level:** high

1. All players should be wearing bathing suits under their clothes. Players take off their shoes and line up along a starting line.

2. Players then drop their pants to their ankles and wait for a starting signal.

3. When the signal is given, players race forward as best as they can.

4. They continue hopping like this on the sand until they fall or until one is too far ahead of the others.

Stomachs In!

This game is played at the beach when children are not wearing shirts. It can be used as a means of player selection.

- **Age:** 4 years and up
- **Approximate Time:** 5 minutes
- **Players:** 2 or more
- **Materials:** none
- **Activity Level:** low

1. Players stand in a circle facing in.

2. One player calls out, "Who can hold her stomach in?" The other players answer, "I can!"

3. The first player then adds, "Let's see!" and all the players suck their stomachs in by holding their breath.

4. Little by little, players will let their stomachs out, either because they get tired or because they can't hold their breath any longer. The last player to give up, that is, the one who can hold her breath the longest, wins.

Fishermen

This game of seek-and-find is played on sand and is fun and exciting for younger children.

- **Age:** 5 years and up
- **Approximate Time:** 10 minutes
- **Players:** 2 or more
- **Materials:** a watch, several small objects (balls, handkerchiefs, bottle caps, etc.)
- **Activity Level:** average

1. Players form two teams of equal number. Members of one team will hide the "fish" and players on the other team will be the fishermen.

2. A playing area is marked and objects to be used as fish are selected. These objects are shown to the fishermen before the game begins.

3. The fishermen turn their backs as the other team hides the fish inside the playing area. When all of the objects are hidden, a signal is given to start the search.

4. While the first team keeps time, the fishermen try to uncover as many fish as possible in two minutes. When time is up, they count all the fish they found, and then the teams switch roles.

44 Crumble

Age: 5 years and up

Approximate Time: 5 minutes

Players: 2 or more

Materials: a small stick for each player, plus an additional one

Activity Level: low

This is a quiet game of skill appropriate for playing after meals. Wet beach sand is best suited for this game.

1. Players gather wet sand from the water's edge and make a small mound. A small stick is then inserted into the top of the mound.

2. An order for play is established, and each player is given a small stick the size of a pencil.

3. Keeping the stick parallel to the ground, players take turn scraping the sand away at the base of the mound. If a player scrapes too little sand, the next player can refuse to take a turn.

4. Players keep scraping until the mound collapses. The last player to scrape before the mound collapses loses and has to build the mound for the next game.

45 Cooperative Drawing

Age: 5 years and up

Approximate Time: 5 minutes

Players: 2 or more

Materials: none

Activity Level: low

In this game, players work together to come up with the silliest drawing possible to make everyone laugh.

1. Players gather on wet sand and establish an order of play.

2. The first player tells the others what she plans to draw, saying, for example, "This is going to be an animal."

3. Then she uses her fingers to draw part of the animal and adds, "And this is his head."

4. Each player has to add another body part to the animal (ears, body, tail, etc.), trying to make it look as funny as possible.

5. The object of this game is to arrive at the most outrageous drawing possible in order to make everyone laugh.

46 Tumbling Worm

In this game, players roll merrily on sand to make another player slide across them.

- **Age:** 5 years and up
- **Approximate Time:** 10 minutes
- **Players:** 6 or more
- **Materials:** none
- **Activity Level:** average

1. Players draw straws to see who will slide on top of the others. The other players lie side by side on the sand about 8 inches apart from each other.

2. The player chosen to slide lies across her

companions, who then begin to roll over in the same direction.

3. When the slider has rolled past a player and the two are no longer touching, that player gets up and runs to lie at the head of the row. The object of the game is to move the sliding player as far as possible.

47 Into the Hole

Players need a lot of skill to win this game of aim.

- **Age:** 6 years and up
- **Approximate Time:** 10 minutes
- **Players:** 3 or more
- **Materials:** 1 stone per player
- **Activity Level:** low

1. Each player receives a stone and an order of play is established. Then a hole is made in the sand about half the size of a soccer ball.

2. A toss line is drawn in the sand about 3 feet away from the hole with players standing behind it. Players then take turns trying to toss their stone into the hole.

3. Players who succeed in hitting the hole pick up their stones and draw a new line in the sand a step back. In the next round, players throw their stones from the new toss line.

4. In each round, players who fail to sink the stone into the hole are eliminated and a new toss line is drawn. The game ends when only one player is left.

48 Sey

This African game is always played on sand. Here one player's power of observation competes with another player's ability to successfully hide an object.

- **Age:** 6 years and up
- **Approximate Time:** 10 minutes
- **Players:** 2
- **Materials:** a small stone
- **Activity Level:** low

1. Two players sit facing each other and draw two concentric circles between them. Each player then digs three holes in the sand directly in front of her.

2. The first player takes the stone or "tibi," and holds it in her hand together with a handful of sand. Slowly she releases the sand into the holes, dropping the stone with the sand so that it is buried in one of the holes.

3. The second player pays close attention, trying to determine into which hole the first player has dropped the stone. When the first player's hands are empty, the other player points to the hole where he thinks the stone is hidden.

4. If he is correct, then it's his turn to hide the stone. If he fails to pick the right hole, then the first player digs another hole to the right of those she has already dug and plays again. Players cannot hide the "tibi" in the same hole twice.

5. Each time a player successfully hides the "tibi," she adds another hole to those she already has. The first player whose holes reach the opponent's holes wins.

49 Treasure Keeper

This is a great game to play in water that is at least knee deep.

- **Age:** 6 years and up
- **Approximate Time:** 10 minutes
- **Players:** 4 or more
- **Materials:** an object that floats
- **Activity Level:** high

1. Players draw straws to see who will be the treasure keeper. The treasure must be an object that floats, such as a beach ball.

2. All of the players get into the water and the treasure keeper lets the treasure float freely. Then she tries to tag a player who will replace her.

3. Everyone tries to take the treasure out of the water without being tagged by the treasure keeper. A player about to be tagged can throw that ball at another player. If that player is hit, he becomes the new treasure keeper.

4. A player who succeeds in getting the treasure out of the water names another player to become the treasure keeper and join the first one. The game ends when there are more keepers than players.

50 Sand Burial

This is a common beach game. One player allows herself to be buried up to her neck and others sculpt the sand around her in the shape she requests.

- **Age:** 6 years and up
- **Approximate Time:** 10 minutes
- **Players:** 2 or more
- **Materials:** none
- **Activity Level:** average

1. A player is chosen to be buried; volunteers are never lacking.

2. The player lies down on the sand and says, for example, "I want to be a mermaid." A towel can be used to cover her to make it more comfortable.

3. The other players pile wet sand around her up to her neck. When she is completely covered, except for her head, players then try to shape the figure she requested.

4. The buried player gives advice on how to mold the shape. When the shape is complete, she gets up and another player is buried.

51 Frog Race

This is a perfect game to be played on soft sand, since players will often land on their bottoms.

- **Age:** 6 years and up
- **Approximate Time:** 10 minutes
- **Players:** 8 or more
- **Materials:** none
- **Activity Level:** average

1. Players draw two lines, a starting and a finish line, about 20 yards apart. Then players divide into teams of four players each.

2. Players on each team stand back to back in a square, interlocking their arms at the elbows. Then they move to the starting line.

3. At the signal, the teams run as fast as they can toward the finish line without letting go of each other. If a team trips and falls, it must get up without releasing its arm locks.

4. The first team to cross the finish line wins, though the fun of the game has more to do with trying to coordinate movements for the run than in arriving first.

Wali-Wali

This highly amusing game can be played on sand or in shallow water.

- **Age:** 7 years and up
- **Approximate Time:** 5 minutes
- **Players:** 9 or more
- **Materials:** none
- **Activity Level:** average

1. Players draw straws to choose who will be tossed. The rest of the players form two parallel lines facing each other.

2. Each player grabs the left forearm of the player in front with her right hand and the right forearm with her left hand, forming a "bridge."

3. The chosen player lies headfirst across the joined arms. The players in line raise and lower their arms rhythmically to move the reclining player forward in small bounces.

4. When the player reaches the end of the line, he is tossed in the water. If the game is played on sand, the last players lower their arms so that he can somersault off.

Bridges

A game of aim in which players take advantage of how easy it is to scrape and dig in the sand.

- **Age:** 7 years and up
- **Approximate Time:** 10 minutes
- **Players:** 2 or more
- **Materials:** a small ball
- **Activity Level:** low

1. Players dig two parallel ditches in the sand about 8 inches apart. The ditches should be about 1 foot wide and about 4 inches deep.

2. In the first ditch, three bridges are made, 8 inches apart, by filling in sections of the ditch with sand. Players then establish an order of play.

3. From a distance of about 15 feet, each player tosses the ball so that it rolls over one of the bridges and falls into the second ditch.

4. Each time a player succeeds, she receives a point and tosses again. Tosses continue until one of the players reaches 10 points.

Throw Your Partner

This is a delightful water game for children in which an adult becomes an improvised trampoline.

- **Age:** 7 years and up
- **Approximate Time:** 10 minutes
- **Players:** 2 or more
- **Materials:** none
- **Activity Level:** high

1. It is important to play this game in water that is at least waist deep to avoid hitting the bottom.

2. The adult will join her hands, interlocking her fingers in front of her, to form a stirrup. The child will put one foot into the stirrup, bending a knee, and will support himself on the adult's shoulders.

3. On the count of "One, two, three, go!" the adult will quickly raise her hands, while the child straightens the leg in the stirrup and flips backward.

4. The game is repeated as many times as the players wish or until the adult is tired. Be sure not to use too much force so that children won't be tossed too far or get hurt.

Mouse, Frog, Cat, Lion

Players pass a ball to each other, slapping it only once with an open hand. Good reflexes are a must in this game.

- **Age:** 8 years and up
- **Approximate Time:** 10 minutes
- **Players:** 4 or more
- **Materials:** a ball
- **Activity Level:** average

1. A 6-foot square is drawn on the sand and divided into four even sections, one for each animal. If there are more than four players, a circle is drawn instead and sections are added for additional animals.

2. Players draw straws to see who will represent each animal. Then they occupy their respective places. The lion starts by passing the ball to another player.

3. The receiving player slaps the ball with her palm to pass it on again. When someone misses, he becomes the mouse, and the other players advance one position.

4. The lion is responsible for putting the ball in play. There should always be at least two passes before passing the ball again to the lion.

Sand Bowling

In this game, sand pins are created and knocked down repeatedly.

- **Age:** 8 years and up
- **Approximate Time:** 5 minutes
- **Players:** 2 or more
- **Materials:** a ball
- **Activity Level:** average

1. Players build two rows of three sand mounds side by side. Behind the mounds, they dig a hole large enough to fit the ball.

2. Players stand about 9 feet from the mounds and take three turns tossing the ball.

3. A player gets two points for each pin she knocks down getting the ball into the hole. She gets one point for each pin she knocks down if she doesn't get the ball into the hole, and ten points if she knocks down all of the pins.

4. After each game the pins are set up again and the next player takes a turn. The player who has the most points at the end of the round wins.

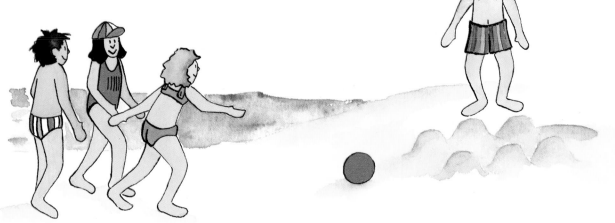

Holes

This is a relaxing game of precision played on wet sand at the water's edge. Players use a straw to pierce a mound of sand.

- **Age:** 8 years and up
- **Approximate Time:** 10 minutes
- **Players:** 2 or more
- **Materials:** a straw
- **Activity Level:** low

1. Players build a mound of wet sand as tall as possible. Then they decide on an order of play.

2. Each player takes a turn poking a straw through the mound.

3. With each player's turn, the mound becomes weaker because of the holes that are being poked into it. This makes it increasingly easy for the mound of sand to collapse.

4. For a hole to be valid, it has to fully pierce the mound so that one can see through it.

5. The game continues until the mound collapses. The last player to insert the straw has to rebuild the mound.

58 Yoté

- **Age:** 8 years and up
- **Approximate Time:** 10 minutes
- **Players:** 2 or more
- **Materials:** 12 stones and 12 sticks
- **Activity Level:** low

1. Players dig six rows of five holes each. Then they draw straws to see who will begin the game. One player uses stones and the other player uses sticks as pawns.

2. Players take turns placing one of their pawns into a hole. They are allowed to move them forward, backward, or

This African game originated in Senegal. The beach is the perfect place to draw the game "board."

sideways. A player does not have to have all of her pawns on the board before she can make a move.

3. If a player's pawn is next to that of an opponent's pawn, she can jump it to capture it. Each time a player captures an opponent's pawn, she takes another one.

4. The game ends when one of the players has fewer than four pawns left. The player who has captured the most pawns wins.

59 Crab Race

This is a fun race in which players have to be fast while maintaining their balance.

- **Age:** 8 years and up
- **Approximate Time:** 5 minutes
- **Players:** 2 or more
- **Materials:** a stone or other small object per player
- **Activity Level:** average

1. Each player receives a stone or other small object and stands at the starting line.

2. All of the players get down "on all fours," stomach up. Once in position, the stone or object is placed on their stomach.

3. At the signal, everyone crab-walks backward, being very careful not to drop the stone.

4. If a player drops the object, she has to place it on her stomach again before continuing on to the finish line. The game can be played with any small object or with cups of water.

GAMES FOR SUMMER

Endless Ribbon

In this race, coordination among all of the team members is important in order to reach the finish line.

- **Age:** 9 years and up
- **Approximate Time:** 10 minutes
- **Players:** 6 or more
- **Materials:** a beach raft for each team
- **Activity Level:** average

1. Players form teams of six and each team receives a beach raft. A starting and finish line are marked.

2. At the signal, all of the players on each team except one lie down next to each other. The standing player places the raft on her teammates.

3. Players roll over to move the raft forward. When the raft has passed over one of the players, that player gets up and runs to the front of the line.

4. Players continue to roll, moving the raft forward until they get to the finish line. This game can also be played to see who gets the farthest without dropping the raft.

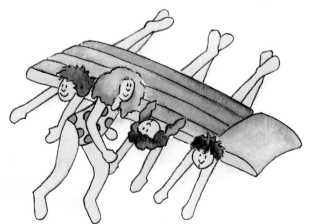
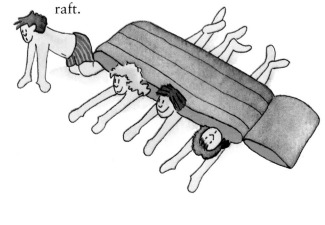

Paso Popas!

A sandy beach is the perfect spot for this game, which is played in many parts of Spain.

- **Age:** 9 years and up
- **Approximate Time:** 10 minutes
- **Players:** 3 or more
- **Materials:** none
- **Activity Level:** average

1. A line is drawn in the sand, with one of the players standing directly behind it in a pony position with her elbows resting on her thighs.

2. The other players take turns jumping over her, placing their hands on her back and swinging their legs around her sides.

When the player jumps, he says "Paso!," except for the last jumper, who says "Paso Popas!"

3. When everyone has jumped, the pony moves a foot farther from the line and everyone jumps again from behind the line. If they wish, they can take a short running start.

4. If one of the players touches the line, does not jump, or touches the pony with any part of his body except his hands, he has to take the pony's place.

Skipping Stones

This game, in which no one gets wet, is fun for both children and adults.

- **Age:** 9 years and up
- **Approximate Time:** 10 minutes
- **Players:** 1 or more
- **Materials:** flat stones
- **Activity Level:** low

1. Players look for several small, flat stones at the water's edge. When they have found the stones, they select an area where there are no swimmers.

2. Players take turns throwing their stones into the water. To make the stone skip, players should hold the stone between the index finger and thumb and fling it forcefully, parallel to the water.

3. Thrown in this way, the stone skims the water, skipping along its surface for a considerable distance. This technique requires practice at first. It is best played when the water is calm.

4. The winner is determined by counting how many consecutive skips a stone makes or how much distance the stone covers in a toss.

The Queen's Throne

This is a popular game well suited for the open spaces of the beach. Falls on the sand are softer than those in other playing areas.

- **Age:** 9 years and up
- **Approximate Time:** 5 minutes
- **Players:** 3 or more
- **Materials:** none
- **Activity Level:** high

1. Players form groups of three and draw straws to see who will be the "queen" on the first round and who will replace her in the next round.

2. The other two players hold their right wrist with their left hand. They use their free right hand to hold the wrist of the companion.

3. The "queen" sits on the square formed by her companions' arms and puts her arms around their shoulders.

4. The "queen" can indicate where she'd like to be carried. If more than one group participates, they can race, or simply take turns playing.

The Giant Rollover

This game of skill and coordination is more appropriate for older children. It is important to be careful and start out slowly to avoid injuries.

- **Age:** 11 years and up
- **Approximate Time:** 5 minutes
- **Players:** 2 or more
- **Materials:** none
- **Activity Level:** average

1. Players form pairs. One of the players lies on the ground face up and the other one stands directly behind her head.

2. Each player grabs the ankles of her companion, so that they both form a loop with their bodies.

3. The player on top rolls over slowly, dragging her companion around and lifting her up.

4. The two players continue rolling in their loop. Loops of three players can also be made.

65 Carry the Jar

In this game, physical strength is more important than speed, even though the object of the game is to see who advances the farthest.

- **Age:** 11 years and up
- **Approximate Time:** 5 minutes
- **Players:** 3 or more
- **Materials:** none
- **Activity Level:** high

1. Players divide into groups of three and stand at the starting line. One of the players crouches down and places her interlocked hands across her stomach.

2. At the signal, each one of her companions takes her by one arm and runs with her in a direction agreed on beforehand.

3. When one of the players on the team yells out "Change!," one of the other players becomes the jar.

4. The object of the game is to see who goes the farthest after two changes, or who reaches the finish line first.

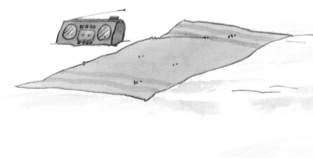

66 Water Towers

This is one of the most popular games on any beach where there are groups of children who are eager to have fun.

- **Age:** 12 years and up
- **Approximate Time:** 10 minutes
- **Players:** 6 or more
- **Materials:** none
- **Activity Level:** high

1. Players get into water at least chest deep to avoid danger when the tower collapses.

2. Two players lift two other players onto their shoulders. Then a third player stands between the first two players to form the base.

3. The players on the shoulders help each other stand up on the three players who form the base.

4. The last player, who is always the lightest, tries to climb on top of the shoulders of the two players on the second tier. Although this is not easy to do, it is a lot of fun.

Games

High temperatures in the summer make trips to the pool with family or friends common outings. To make these trips more appealing and to ensure fun, it is wise to have a number of water games ready to play to make the most of the time spent at the pool.

22 water games that will amuse children. Playing in water is special. We can swim, do somersaults, snorkel, and dive. It is necessary for adults to always accompany children to the pool and to make them aware of the pool rules before they begin to play.

67 Water Relay

This very easy team game played out of the pool helps make getting into the water more fun.

- **Age:** 5 years and up
- **Approximate Time:** 10 minutes
- **Players:** 5 or more
- **Materials:** a plastic cup per player
- **Activity Level:** low

1. Each player receives a plastic cup. Then players sit in a line, each one between the legs of the player behind.

2. The first player fills his cup with water and holds it on his head with one hand. The next player holds the rim of her cup between her teeth.

3. The first player tilts his head back and without turning around tries to pour the water from his cup into the cup of the player behind him. That player tries to catch the water without spilling it.

4. When a player has passed the water, he gets up and goes to the end of the line and waits to catch it when it is his turn again. The game ends when there is no more water left in the cups.

Crocodiles and Turtles

This is a game of tag for pools that have areas of very shallow water.

- **Age:** 5 years and up
- **Approximate Time:** 10 minutes
- **Players:** 4 or more
- **Materials:** none
- **Activity Level:** average

1. Players draw straws to see who will be the crocodile. The other players are turtles. The crocodile goes to one corner of the pool and the turtles to the opposite.

2. The crocodile chases the turtles lying face down in the water, holding himself up by placing his hands on the bottom of the pool. The turtles run from the crocodile in a squatting position.

3. When a crocodile catches a turtle, the turtle becomes a crocodile, too, and joins in the chase of other turtles.

4. A turtle that successfully reaches the crocodile's corner can turn a crocodile back into a turtle. The turtle then has to return to his corner without being tagged before he can continue playing.

69 The Water Wall

This game can be played in water that is either ankle deep or chest deep. The age of the players will depend on the depth of the water.

- **Age:** 6 years and up
- **Approximate Time:** 10 minutes
- **Players:** 6 or more
- **Materials:** a ball (any size)
- **Activity Level:** average

1. Two players are chosen to pass the ball to each other; they stand about 30 feet apart.

2. The other players line up in a single file, forming a wall between

the two players passing the ball, and try to intercept the ball as it flies by.

3. The players who form the wall can move only sideways to catch the ball.

4. When a player from the wall succeeds in catching the ball, she becomes a passer. The last player who touched the ball moves to the head of the wall.

70 Underwater Messages

This game always surprises children who are able to keep their heads under the water.

- **Age:** 7 years and up
- **Approximate Time:** 5 minutes
- **Players:** 5 or more
- **Materials:** none
- **Activity Level:** low

1. Players hold hands and form a circle in the water. One of them says, "Who can guess what I say?"

2. Then everyone crouches down, with their heads underwater. The player who asked

the question says a word very loudly underwater.

3. The other players try very hard to understand the word. Once the word has been said, they all take their heads out of the water.

4. Each player says what he thinks he heard under the water. The one who guesses the word correctly gets to say the next word. If no one guesses, the process is repeated.

71 Tube Fishing

This racing game should be played in areas of shallow water where it will not inconvenience other swimmers.

- **Age:** 7 years and up
- **Approximate Time:** 10 minutes
- **Players:** 2 or more
- **Materials:** 3 inflatable tubes per player
- **Activity Level:** high

1. Before beginning the game, the inflatable tubes should be placed in the water.

2. Players gather at the side of the pool and, at a signal, run to catch as many of the tubes as possible.

3. Players cannot catch the tubes using their hands or arms. They can use only their head and feet.

4. When there are no more uncaught tubes, all players return to the side of the pool with their catch. If a player drops one of the tubes, another player can quickly try to pick it up.

72 Somersaults

This is a game in which children who are able to swim underwater can show off their sense of balance and agility.

- **Age:** 7 years and up
- **Approximate Time:** 5 minutes
- **Players:** 2 or more
- **Materials:** none
- **Activity Level:** average

1. Players gather at a place in the pool where the water comes up to the middle of their chests.

2. Players take turns doing as many somersaults as possible, allowing only their feet to touch the bottom of the pool.

3. The other players count the number of somersaults out loud and watch to be sure they are done correctly and that players don't fall over to the side.

4. When a player gets tired or dizzy, she stops and the next player takes a turn. The player who performs the most consecutive somersaults wins.

73 Floating Basket

A water game in which the strength of teams is kept even by having scorers switch teams.

- **Age:** 7 years and up
- **Approximate Time:** 10 minutes
- **Players:** 6 or more
- **Materials:** 2 inflatable tubes, one plastic ball
- **Activity Level:** average

1. Players divide into two teams of equal number. Then each team receives an inflatable tube that will be used as their basket.

2. Each team floats their basket on one side of the pool, and the players spread out over the designated playing area. The goal is to put the ball into the opponents' basket.

3. When a player has the ball, she cannot move, but instead has to pass it to a teammate. While playing, players cannot touch the baskets.

4. If a player makes a basket, she scores a point for her team and then switches teams. The game continues for a specified time or until players are tired.

Water Challenge

A game of strength in which players try to move their opponent backward by kicking the water with their feet.

- **Age:** 7 years and up
- **Approximate Time:** 5 minutes
- **Players:** 2 or more
- **Materials:** a large inflatable tube
- **Activity Level:** high

1. Two players position themselves face to face, holding onto an inflatable tube with both hands.

2. Both say "1, 2, 3, go!" at the same time and start kicking the water with their feet to propel themselves forward.

3. They continue kicking their feet until one gives up or moves backward.

4. A variation of the game consists of kicking sideways to turn the tube around rather than move it forward.

The Pot

In this game of tag, players are safe from "It" only when they are touching the side of the pool.

- **Age:** 7 years and up
- **Approximate Time:** 10 minutes
- **Players:** 4 or more
- **Materials:** none
- **Activity Level:** average

1. "It" positions herself away from the sides of the pool. The rest of the players are touching the sides.

2. From her position in the middle, "It" yells "Everybody change!" At that point, everyone has to move to the other side of the pool.

3. "It" can tag anyone who is not touching a side. Players have to stay at least 15 feet away from the corners of the pool.

4. A player who is tagged also becomes "It." The game ends when there are more players doing the chasing than being chased.

76 Neptune

- **Age:** 7 years and up
- **Approximate Time:** 10 minutes
- **Players:** 3 or more
- **Materials:** none
- **Activity Level:** average

1. Players draw straws to see who will be Neptune and who will be the shark. The rest of the players will be fish.

2. The shark chases the fish all over the pool. When the shark catches a fish, they switch roles.

In this game, the player who is Neptune is a safe haven for all of the fish being chased by the shark.

3. Fish are considered safe when they touch the hand of the player who is Neptune. If at some point there are too many fish touching him, or if the fish are staying around him too long, Neptune can decide to drop underwater.

4. When Neptune is submerged, he is no longer a safe haven and the fish can be tagged by the shark. Every so often the player who is playing Neptune is replaced. The game continues until players tire or decide to play another game.

77 Shark

- **Age:** 8 years and up
- **Approximate Time:** 10 minutes
- **Players:** 4 or more
- **Materials:** none
- **Activity Level:** high

1. One of the players is chosen to be the shark in the first round of the game. The others try to avoid the shark.

2. The shark chooses a corner as his home base and sets out to tag the others. To tag someone, the shark has to swim underwater and grab the player by the ankles.

3. When the shark tags a player, she takes him to her home base. The player must stay there until one of his companions frees him by touching his hand.

4. When the shark has two or three fish at her home base, she trades places with the first fish she caught. If there are a lot of players, more than one shark can be chosen.

This is a game for children who can swim, because to tag a companion players have to be able to swim a distance underwater.

Fish the Handkerchiefs

- **Age:** 8 years and up
- **Approximate Time:** 10 minutes
- **Players:** 4 or more
- **Materials:** a handkerchief or cap per player
- **Activity Level:** high

1. Before starting, an allotted time is designated to play the game. All players put a handkerchief or cap on their head. Then they mill about the pool.

2. At the signal "Fish the handkerchiefs!" each player tries to seize the handkerchief or cap from a companion's head while holding on to his own.

In this game, players try to seize the handkerchiefs or caps from other players' heads while trying to keep their own on.

3. If a player loses her handkerchief or cap, she can continue playing. However, the moment she captures another player's handkerchief or cap, she must place it on her head. Players are not allowed to hide underwater to avoid having their handkerchiefs or caps taken.

4. Once the allotted time is up, players come together to see who has acquired the most handkerchiefs or caps.

79 Bumping Boats

For this game, each player needs a raft large enough to sit on. Inner tubes are ideal.

- **Age:** 7 years and up
- **Approximate Time:** 10 minutes
- **Players:** 2 or more
- **Materials:** a large raft or inner tube
- **Activity Level:** average

1. Each player grabs a raft and heads for the pool. At the signal, players sit on their rafts.

2. Using only their hands and feet, players try to propel themselves toward other players and attempt to bump and flip their rafts over.

3. When players bump into each other, each tries to knock the other over with their hands and feet. If a player knocks another one into the water, he must move away.

4. Players who have been knocked into the water cannot flip others until they are back on their rafts. The game continues until players get tired.

80 Starfish

Players need to demonstrate self-control in order to float on their backs as long as they can.

- **Age:** 8 years and up
- **Approximate Time:** 5 minutes
- **Players:** 2 or more
- **Materials:** none
- **Activity Level:** low

1. Players form a circle in water that is at least waist deep.

2. At a signal, all players lie on their backs with arms extended and float like starfish.

3. In order to float, players need to keep their backs straight, stick their chests out, and try to keep in as much air as possible.

4. When players get tired or are no longer able to float, they stand up. The player that floats the longest is the winner.

Water Jumps

- **Age:** 8 years and up
- **Approximate Time:** 5 minutes
- **Players:** 4 or more
- **Materials:** none
- **Activity Level:** average

In this follow-the-leader pool game, players jump into the water from the side of the pool in different and creative ways. It is important for players to be sure that no one is in their way.

1. Players gather at the side of the pool in an area where there are no other swimmers and where the water is deep enough to jump without getting hurt.

2. An order for jumping is decided and players line up accordingly. The first player jumps into the water, showing how all of the others must jump.

3. Some common jumps are the cannonball (with legs held tightly to the jumper's chest), the needle (keeping as straight as possible), or head first, watching carefully to see where the player will land.

4. When all of the players have jumped, following the lead of the first player, the first player moves to the end of the line and the second player leads the next round of jumps.

Sunken Treasure

- **Age:** 8 years and up
- **Approximate Time:** 10 minutes
- **Players:** 3 or more
- **Materials:** a small object that can get wet
- **Activity Level:** average

In this game, players try to retrieve the sunken treasure from the bottom of the pool. This is a wonderful game for those who are comfortable swimming underwater.

1. A sinkable object is chosen to be the treasure. A painted rock is perfect for this game.

2. Everyone stands at the edge of the pool while one of the players tosses the treasure into the water.

3. When the treasure hits the water, all of the players jump into the water, trying to retrieve it.

4. Players swim underwater to find the treasure. The player who finds it first retrieves it and brings it back to the edge of the pool where it will be tossed back into the water for another round.

Water Tunnel

This is a fun game that tests players' ability to swim underwater and hold their breath.

- **Age:** 9 years and up
- **Approximate Time:** 10 minutes
- **Players:** 4 or more
- **Materials:** none
- **Activity Level:** average

1. An order is decided and players line up in single file by the side of the pool. The first player dives in and, upon emerging from the water, stands with his legs apart facing the other players.

2. The second player jumps into the water and swims under the legs of the first player. When the second player comes up, he assumes the same open-legged stance as the first player, standing 2 feet behind him.

3. Players continue jumping in, swimming under their companions' legs, and taking their place at the end of the line. If a player is unable to swim the entire line underwater, he can walk.

4. When the last player has jumped into the water and swum under the tunnel, he signals the first player in line who drops underwater and starts the game over again by swimming through the tunnel to the other end.

The Water Snake

This is a game best played by experienced swimmers with very good coordination.

- **Age:** 9 years and up
- **Approximate Time:** 10 minutes
- **Players:** 8 or more
- **Materials:** none
- **Activity Level:** high

1. Players divide into groups of four. Then they line up with their backs against the side of the pool.

2. When one of the players gives the starting signal, players from each team grab on to each others' waists, forming a "serpent."

3. All of the "serpents" swim to the opposite side of the pool. Only the head swimmers on each team can use their arms and legs to swim. The players behind can use only their legs.

4. If one of the "serpents" comes apart in the middle of the race, it cannot continue racing until it has joined again. The first team to cross the pool wins.

85 Fish and Net

In this game the "fish" need to pay close attention to the "fishermen," who at any minute can form a net to trap them.

- **Age:** 9 years and up
- **Approximate Time:** 10 minutes
- **Players:** 8 or more
- **Materials:** none
- **Activity Level:** average

1. Three players are chosen to be the fishermen, while the rest of the players mill about the pool in shallow water.

2. The fishermen try to trap the fish. To catch a fish, the fishermen need to form a net of at least three players holding hands.

3. If there are fewer than three players forming a net, the fishermen cannot catch a fish. Trapped fish become fishermen.

4. The game is played until all of the fish are caught. The three fish caught first are fishermen in the next game.

86 Water Goal

The sides of the pool are the goal lines in this fast game whose pace must be sustained.

- **Age:** 9 years and up
- **Approximate Time:** 10 minutes
- **Players:** 6 or more
- **Materials:** a ball that floats
- **Activity Level:** average

1. Players are divided into two equal teams. Each team is assigned a side of the pool as their goal line.

2. The ball is put into play in the middle of the pool, and each team tries to touch the other's goal line with the ball in order to score a point.

3. Players cannot hold the ball with their hands. To move the ball, players must either throw it, push it with their hand underwater, or swim with it between their arms.

4. When a player reaches her opponent's goal with the ball, she gains a point. If while shooting for the goal, the ball is tossed out of the pool, no point is scored.

87 Bucket Ball

This fun and exciting team game for older children combines basketball with water polo.

- **Age:** 10 years and up
- **Approximate Time:** 10 minutes
- **Players:** 6 or more
- **Materials:** 1 tennis ball, 2 beach pails
- **Activity Level:** average

1. Players divide into two teams. Each team places its pail on one side of the pool directly across from the other.

2. Each player tries to toss the tennis ball into the opposing team's pail to score a point.

3. Players can use only their hands to handle the ball and their feet cannot touch the bottom of the pool while passing the ball. Once they have passed the ball, they can touch the bottom again.

4. When shooting at the pail, players cannot be touching the bottom of the pool. This is what makes the game difficult. This game is played to five points.

88 Seahorses

There are no winners or losers in this water fight, which players continue to play until they get tired.

- **Age:** 11 years and up
- **Approximate Time:** 10 minutes
- **Players:** 4 or more
- **Materials:** none
- **Activity Level:** high

1. Players form pairs, with one being the horse and the other the jockey. Afterward, they switch roles.

2. The jockeys stand with their legs apart so that the horses can lift them onto their shoulders.

3. Once in this position, players move to water that is chest deep so there is no danger if they fall.

4. Pairs try to knock other pairs over. When a jockey falls, he must get back on his horse immediately to continue playing.

GAMES FOR SUMMER

Games

Day camps and overnight camps, parks, and large groups of friends provide enjoyable opportunities for playing interactive team games. The only material needed for playing is a ball.

12 team games that test players' skills, reflexes, and ability to play together. This section provides a variety of ways for active group participation at summer camps and during camp-outs and outings, under the supervision of adults.

89) The Roll

Players on one team try to cross a circle formed by the other team without getting caught inside.

- **Age:** 7 years and up
- **Approximate Time:** 10 minutes
- **Players:** 10 or more
- **Materials:** none
- **Activity Level:** average

1. One player is selected as game leader while the others divide into two teams. One team forms a circle, raising arms and joining hands.

2. At the leader's signal, the other team tries to cross through the circle by entering and exiting under the players' raised arms.

3. When the leader shouts "Down!" the team forming the circle lowers its arms, trapping players inside. Those players then join the circle.

4. The circle gets larger with each round and therefore more difficult to cross. When all of the players are caught, the teams switch roles.

90) Balance

In this game, players keep switching teams to keep the pull on the rope balanced.

- **Age:** 7 years and up
- **Approximate Time:** 5 minutes
- **Players:** 8 or more
- **Materials:** a rope
- **Activity Level:** low

1. Players divide into two teams, with their weight distributed as evenly as possible.

2. Players on each team line up in single file facing each other.

3. Once the teams are in place holding the rope, the players shout "Up!" and everyone takes a step forward at the same time without letting go of the rope. Then they shout "Back" and they all lean back, putting all of their weight on the rope they're holding.

4. The object of the game is to keep the two teams balanced. If they are not, a player moves to the lighter team and they try again.

To the Jungle!

In this fast-paced and fun game for younger children, everyone has to listen carefully as the name of their animal is called out.

- **Age:** 7 years and up
- **Approximate Time:** 10 minutes
- **Players:** 9 or more
- **Materials:** a small ball
- **Activity Level:** average

1. Players divide into three or more teams, with at least three players per team. Then teams line up around the ball like blades of a fan.

2. A game leader is selected who will decide which animals the teams will have. All teams will have the same animals, with each player being assigned one.

3. The leader calls out the name of an animal. Players on each team who have been assigned that animal run around the outside of the circle. When they get back to their team, they run under the legs of their teammates to grab the ball.

4. The first player to reach the ball wins a point. If the leader shouts "To the Jungle!" all the players run a lap, and the last player on each team to get back to his position races to get the ball.

Bowling

An easygoing team game in which players must avoid being hit by a ball their opponents toss at them.

- **Age:** 7 years and up
- **Approximate Time:** 30 minutes
- **Players:** 8 or more
- **Materials:** a ball
- **Activity Level:** average

1. Players look for a flat area to play and then divide into two teams. Teams line up facing each other.

2. One player rolls the ball, trying to touch a player on the opposite team. Players cannot move, except to jump up with their feet together to avoid the ball.

3. If the ball touches a player, that player has to sit on the ground with his feet toward the opposing team. If the sitting player succeeds in touching a rolling ball with his feet, he can stand up again.

4. On each round, players take turns rolling the ball. However, only those who are standing up can do so. The game ends when an entire team is sitting on the ground.

The Pitcher

This team game is a favorite of children. Players can spend large amounts of time totally absorbed in this competition.

- **Age:** 7 years and up
- **Approximate Time:** 30 minutes
- **Players:** 8 or more
- **Materials:** a small ball, chalk
- **Activity Level:** average

1. The playing field is drawn by marking a circle for the batter and another for the pitcher about 6 feet away. A course of five or more bases is also marked.

2. The first team lines up behind the batter while members of the other team scatter around the field. The pitcher tosses the ball to the batter, who hits it with his fist.

3. The team members around the field try to catch the ball and throw it back to the pitcher, who must remain inside her circle. Meanwhile, the batter and other players who have reached a base circle the bases.

4. When the pitcher catches the ball, he shouts "Pitcher!" and the runners who have reached a base have to hold there. If they are caught off base, they are eliminated. The next player comes up to hit and the process continues.

5. If a player succeeds in circling the bases, he can save an eliminated player on his team. If a player catches a fly ball, it is his team's turn to bat.

6. When all of the players on a team have been eliminated, teams switch roles and the game continues.

94 Chinese Dragons

A team game of tag in which players form a dragon by holding on to each other's waists.

- **Age:** 8 years and up
- **Approximate Time:** 10 minutes
- **Players:** 8 or more
- **Materials:** none
- **Activity Level:** average

1. Players are divided into teams of four or five, and each team forms a dragon by lining up and grabbing the person in front by the waist.

2. Dragons stand at the far corners of a field. At a signal, the dragons set out trying to tag the other dragons.

3. If the player at the head of the dragon touches the player at the tail of another dragon, the latter is eliminated. The last surviving player is the winner.

4. A variation of the game consists of having the tail player of a dragon, when tagged, move to the head of the dragon who tagged him, making the game last longer.

95 Messages Without Words

In this game, players have to pass on to their teammates a message given to them by the game leader. However, they have to do so silently.

- **Age:** 8 years and up
- **Approximate Time:** 10 minutes
- **Players:** 8 or more
- **Materials:** none
- **Activity Level:** average

1. Players divide into two teams of equal numbers. The two teams then stand 25 feet apart. The game leader stands in the middle.

2. One player from each team approaches the game leader to get a word.

3. Players convey the word by pantomime, without uttering anything aloud; that is, they can mouth the word or use their hand to draw it in the air. The player who guesses the word will get the next word from the game leader.

4. Teams continue guessing words until all words chosen by the leader have been guessed. The first team to do so wins.

GAMES FOR SUMMER

Kick Ball

In this game, players have to kick the ball hard enough for them to run around the bases before the other team catches it and puts it into a basket.

- **Age:** 8 years and up
- **Approximate Time:** 30 minutes
- **Players:** 10 or more
- **Materials:** a ball, chalk, a bucket
- **Activity Level:** average

1. An area for the kicker and a course for as many bases as there are players are marked on a playing field. Then a circle is drawn in the middle of the field and a bucket is placed there.

2. Players are divided into two teams: the kicking team and the receiving team. A player from the first team kicks the ball and runs around the bases. She can keep running until the other team puts the ball in the bucket.

3. The second team tries to catch the ball and put it into the bucket. When they are successful, they yell "Bucket!" and players from the kicking team who are not on a base are out.

4. A player on the receiving team can throw the ball at another player who is running around the bases and is between bases instead of tossing it into the bucket. If the runner is tagged by the ball, he is eliminated.

5. More than one player can be on a same base at the same time. However, if a team doesn't have any kickers left, the round is over and teams switch roles.

Broom Ball

A ball game in which players use brooms to score points.

- **Age:** 8 years and up
- **Approximate Time:** 30 minutes
- **Players:** 10 or more
- **Materials:** 1 broom per player, a ball, chalk
- **Activity Level:** high

1. Players form two teams and mark off a playing area about the size of an indoor soccer field. The playing area is divided into two, and each team lines up on its side of the field.

2. Each team tries to advance the ball across the opponent's end line in order to score a point. After a team scores a point, the ball goes over to the other team.

3. The players can touch the ball only with their brooms. Players can pass the ball to each other, but if anyone touches it with his feet, the ball automatically goes over to the opposing team.

4. The game is played for a specified amount of time or until a team scores ten points.

98 Turtles

A game in which the players form a turtle by getting on all fours and placing a blanket or mat over their backs.

- **Age:** 8 years and up
- **Approximate Time:** 10 minutes
- **Players:** 8 or more
- **Materials:** a blanket or mat per team
- **Activity Level:** average

1. Players divide into groups of four and take positions at opposite ends of the playing area.

2. Players on each team get down on all fours and cover themselves with a blanket or mat to form the turtles.

3. The turtles then move toward each other and try to rip off their "shells."

4. If a turtle's shell falls off, it has to go back to its starting position to put it on again. If another turtle rips it off, the turtle who loses the shell is eliminated. The last surviving turtle is the winner.

99 Poison Kick

To avoid being eliminated, players must dodge the ball kicked by the opposing team.

- **Age:** 8 years and up
- **Approximate Time:** 30 minutes
- **Players:** 10 or more
- **Materials:** a ball, chalk
- **Activity Level:** average

1. Players form two teams. Then they draw a playing field 15 feet by 10 feet, and divide it into two. Each team retreats to its side of the field.

2. Players kick the ball from their side of the field, trying to hit their opponents. If the ball touches an opponent, that player is eliminated and must retreat outside the playing field.

3. Eliminated players cannot kick the ball, but they can retrieve balls out of bounds and pass them to their teammates so they can kick them.

4. A ball will eliminate a player only if, after it has touched a player, it stays in bounds. The game is played until all players on a team are eliminated.

GAMES FOR ALL YEAR

The Goalpost

An exciting game in which a player acts like a basket by standing on a stool.

- **Age:** 9 years and up
- **Approximate Time:** 30 minutes
- **Players:** 10 or more
- **Materials:** 1 ball, 2 stools, chalk
- **Activity Level:** high

1. Two stools are placed 15 feet inside the end boundaries of a playing area the size of an indoor soccer field. A circle 6 feet in diameter is drawn around each stool.

2. Players are divided into two teams. Each team chooses one of its players to stand on a stool on the opponent's side of the field as a goalpost. Players draw straws to see which team will start and put the ball in play.

3. Players can pass the ball to each other with their hands, but they cannot pass it more than three times. If they bounce the ball, they lose it to the other team.

4. Each time a player succeeds in passing the ball to his teammate in the goalpost position, he scores a point. The player in the post position cannot step off the stool to catch the ball and players cannot enter the circle around the post.

Alphabetical Index

Name of the Game	Page	Age (from)	Approximate Time	Players	Material	Activity
A-E-I-O-U	18	9	5 min.	4 or more	yes	average
Alphabet Objects	26	6	10 min.	2 or more	no	low
Balance	70	7	5 min.	8 or more	yes	low
Ball Catch	16	8	10 min.	2 or more	yes	average
Balloon Fight	9	5	10 min.	4 or more	yes	high
Balloon Toss	13	7	5 min.	2 or more	yes	low
Barabú	15	7	10 min.	5 or more	no	average
Bench, The	10	5	5 min.	7 or more	yes	high
Bocce	11	6	10 min.	2 or more	yes	low
Bottle Keeper	19	9	30 min.	7 or more	yes	average
Bouncy Bounce	17	8	5 min.	1 or more	yes	average
Bowling	71	7	30 min.	8 or more	yes	average
Bridges	44	7	10 min.	2 or more	yes	low
Broom Ball	75	8	30 min.	10 or more	yes	high
Bucket Ball	67	10	10 min.	6 or more	yes	average
Bumping Boats	62	7	10 min.	2 or more	yes	average
Carry the Jar	51	11	5 min.	3 or more	no	high
Chinese Dragons	73	8	10 min.	8 or more	no	average
Code	28	7	10 min.	2 or more	no	low
Colors and Sizes	25	6	5 min.	2 or more	no	low
Combined Letters	31	8	5 min.	2 or more	no	low
Cooperative Drawing	38	5	5 min.	2 or more	no	low
Crab Race	47	8	5 min.	2 or more	yes	average
Crocodiles and Turtles	55	5	10 min.	4 or more	no	average
Crumble	38	5	5 min.	2 or more	yes	low
Dog, Cat, Mouse . . .	32	8	5 min.	2 or more	no	low
Elastic Ropes	11	6	10 min.	3 or more	yes	average
Endless Ribbon	48	9	10 min.	6 or more	yes	average
Fill the Bucket	12	6	10 min.	10 or more	yes	average
Fish and Net	66	9	10 min.	8 or more	no	average
Fish the Handkerchiefs	61	8	10 min.	4 or more	yes	high
Fishermen	37	5	10 min.	2 or more	yes	average
Floating Basket	58	7	10 min.	6 or more	yes	average
Frog Race	42	6	10 min.	8 or more	no	average
Giant Rollover, The	50	11	5 min.	2 or more	no	average
Goalpost, The	77	9	30 min.	10 or more	yes	high
Hide-and-Seek	14	7	10 min.	5 or more	no	average
Holes	46	8	10 min.	2 or more	yes	low
Hoop Roll	17	8	10 min.	1 or more	yes	average
Into the Hole	39	6	10 min.	3 or more	yes	low
Kick Ball	74	8	30 min.	10 or more	yes	average
License Plate Contest	33	9	30 min.	2 or more	no	low
License Plates and Words	30	7	10 min.	2 or more	no	low
Limping Roosters	12	6	5 min.	2 or more	no	average
Line of Letters	32	9	10 min.	2 or more	no	low
Messages Without Words	73	8	10 min.	8 or more	no	average
Mouse, Frog, Cat, Lion	45	8	10 min.	4 or more	yes	average
Neptune	60	7	10 min.	3 or more	no	average

Name of the Game	Page	Age (from)	Approximate Time	Players	Material	Activity
On to Rome	18	9	30 min.	8 or more	yes	high
Palm Clap	27	6	5 min.	2	no	low
Paso Popas!	48	9	10 min.	3 or more	no	average
Pass the Water	10	6	10	5 or more	yes	low
Penguin Race	36	4	5 min.	2 or more	no	high
Pitcher, The	72	7	30 min.	8 or more	yes	average
Poison Kick	76	8	30 min.	10 or more	yes	average
Pot, The	59	7	10 min.	4 or more	no	average
Propeller	20	9	5 min.	2	yes	high
Pull the Stick	13	7	5 min.	2 players	yes	average
Puzzle Hunt	21	10	30 min.	6 or more	yes	average
Queen's Throne, The	50	9	5 min.	3 or more	no	high
Roll, The	70	7	10 min.	10 or more	no	average
Sand Bowling	46	8	5 min.	2 or more	yes	average
Sand Burial	42	6	10 min.	2 or more	no	average
Say It Again	27	6	10 min.	3 or more	no	low
Seahorses	67	11	10 min.	4 or more	no	high
Sey	40	6	10 min.	2	yes	low
Shark	60	8	10 min.	4 or more	no	high
Skipping Stones	49	9	10 min.	1 or more	yes	low
Somersaults	57	7	5 min.	2 or more	no	average
Speeding Hoop	14	7	10 min.	2 or more	yes	average
Starfish	62	8	5 min.	2 or more	no	low
Stealing Ground	21	11	10 min.	2 or more	yes	low
Stomachs In!	36	4	5 min.	2 or more	no	low
Sunken Treasure	63	8	10 min.	3 or more	yes	average
Three Questions	26	6	10 min.	2 or more	no	low
Throw Your Partner	44	7	10 min.	2 or more	no	high
To the Jungle!	71	7	10 min.	9 or more	yes	average
Travel Magazine	24	5	10 min.	2 or more	yes	low
Treasure Keeper	41	6	10 min.	4 or more	yes	high
Tube Fishing	57	7	10 min.	2 or more	yes	high
Tumbling Worm	39	5	10 min.	6 or more	no	average
Turtles	76	8	10 min.	8 or more	yes	average
Underwater Messages	56	7	5 min.	5 or more	no	low
Wali-Wali	43	7	5 min.	9 or more	no	average
Water Bowling	20	9	10 min.	2 or more	yes	high
Water Carrier	8	4	10 min.	2 or more	yes	average
Water Challenge	59	7	5 min.	2 or more	yes	high
Water Goal	66	9	10 min.	6 or more	yes	average
Water Jumps	63	8	5 min.	4 or more	no	average
Water Relay	54	5	10 min.	5 or more	yes	low
Water Slide, The	8	5	5 min.	2 or more	yes	average
Water Snake, The	65	9	10 min.	8 or more	no	high
Water Towers	51	12	10 min.	6 or more	no	high
Water Tunnel	64	9	10 min.	4 or more	no	average
Water Wall, The	56	6	10 min.	6 or more	yes	average
What Should We Put in There?	29	7	5 min.	2 or more	no	low
Word Chain	28	6	10 min.	2 or more	no	low
Words and Letters	30	7	5 min.	2 or more	no	low
Wounded, Grave, and Dead	16	8	10 min.	4 or more	yes	average
Yoté	47	8	10 min.	2 or more	yes	low

Bibliography

Balser, Richard. *Are We There Yet? Travel Games for Kids*. New York: Random House, 1991.

Bartl, Almuth. *Eddie's Finger Quiz Books* (six in the series). Hauppauge, NY: Barron's Educational Series, Inc., 2000.

Belka, David. *Teaching Children Games: Becoming a Master Teacher*. Champaign, IL: Human Kinetics Publications, 1994.

Childre, Doc Lew, et al. *Teaching Children to Love: 80 Games & Fun Activities for Raising Balanced Children in Unbalanced Times*. Boulder Creek, CA: Planetary Publications, 1996.

Collis, Len. *Card Games for Children*. Hauppauge, NY: Barron's Educational Series, Inc., 1989.

Feldman, Jean R. *The Complete Handbook of Indoor and Outdoor Games and Activities for Young Children*. Upper Saddle River, NJ: Prentice Hall, 1994.

Herd, Meg. *Learn and Play in the Garden*. Hauppauge, NY: Barron's Educational Series, Inc., 1997.

Kirchner, Glenn. *Children's Games from Around the World*. Needham Heights, MA: Allyn & Bacon, 2000.

Perez, Eulalia. *100 Best Games*. Hauppauge, NY: Barron's Educational Series, Inc., 2000.

Roopnarine, Jaipaul (ed.), et al. *Children's Play in Diverse Cultures*. New York: State University of New York, 1994.

Stott, Dorothy M. *The Big Book of Games*. New York: Dutton Books, 1998.

Swan, Ann. *How to Make Games for Children: A Handbook of Noncompetitive Games Written for Parents & Educators for Use with Children Ages 2 Thru 12*. Woodinville, WA: Pound Publishing, 1986.

Acknowledgments

To Maqui, for everything; to my parents who never got tired of playing with us; to ATZAR, Association of Game Libraries of Catalonia; to Game Libraries La Guineu and Apatam; and to IOCEW, Coordinator of Game Enterprises.